BE ENCOURAGED

BE ENCOURAGED

BE Encouraged

LILIA HART

CULTURED PEACE SERVICES LLC IMPRINT PUBLISHING
CHARLOTTE, NC

Contents

Part II.
LET IT GO

Part III.
SERENITY

My Reason

Things happen in life to bring you closer to *The Most High* this is a little piece of me and what I went through that I wanted to share with you guys. Before I go into it I just want to say all praises, glory, and honor belong to *The Most High* for deliverance & salvation. This is for his mercy and the glory is not mine at all. I was able to write this from the things I went through to get where I'm at now. I ask for the strength to write this and to stick with it. Fear and procrastination kept me from this for a very long time but here I am, I finally did it. Don't give up on yourself or *The Most High* because he will not give up on you. Now, I'm not going to give you my whole life story I'm going to share with you why I decided to write this. At times a woman or a man just needs encouraging words to get them through the day, week, or maybe even the hour. I have had my share of trials and tribulations. I am not someone sharing this information with you that has it all together but know that no matter what you go through you can get back up again.

Quite a few years ago I found myself in an undesireable situation. I didn't know how to get out of it. What I thought was love was beating me mentally and physically and I thought it was ok for so long because I heard "I do this because I love you" a lot. I was hurt in what I thought was a safe place, I was abused almost every other day, called out my name, and more. I was so in love with the man that I painted him to be something he was not. I overlooked a lot of things with him that were clearly toxic but I stayed, I thought he would change. I began doing drugs to keep my mind at ease and to escape the fear of being with him and what he would do to me. I was smoking and drinking to keep myself level-headed. Let me say you can do all the things in the world to keep a man around and show him that you love him and want to be with him but if he doesn't want to change he's not. I stayed through blows from objects, his fist, and hands, I stayed through words that cut so deep but would push them to the back of my head because I would tell myself it'll get better but in reality, it was only getting worse. I stayed and put up with so much until I finally got the strength to leave but it was not an easy walk at all.

At that time I was about 155 maybe 60 pounds and in a matter of two weeks, I was 121 pounds. I wouldn't eat, I couldn't sleep without waking up crying. My mind was everywhere and my heart was broken in so many pieces it was sore and weak. I had never in my life felt something so hurtful and deep like that. I felt like I had just lost a very big piece of me and was shattered. I did what I could to get myself back on the right path but I fell deeper into depression & anger. I wasn't myself at all and I knew that I just didn't care anymore. I didn't look the same and my spirit was off and sad. I was in a very dark place and it was getting darker by the minute I felt like I was alone and needed help badly. I wanted revenge because everything was hurting and I felt like nobody cared but our plans and *The All-Mighty* plans are not the same. *The Most High* began my process of healing around 2019. In that time, I got closer to him and he showed me real love, joy, and peace and all I needed was him and I had to forgive and move forward. Matthew 6:14-15; [14] For if ye forgive men their trespasses, your heavenly Father will also forgive you. [15] But if ye forgive not men their trespasses, neither will your Father forgive your trespasses. If you are in a low place and feel like you can't get out you can and you will. Nothing happens overnight but with fasting, prayer, faith, being obedient, living your life in his standard his will not your own, and keeping his commandments, statutes, and laws.

You can make it through by keeping him first and everything else will fall into place. I made it and I'm still making it because of the living God the miracle worker. He said in his word nothing is too big for him. When we think things are going out of whack and it looks bad everything is really beginning to fall into place no matter how bad it may seem. I am now married to an amazing man. I have a beautiful family and we are doing very well. All Praises to *The Most High*. I wanted to share some things to keep in your hearts and minds throughout the day. If you feel like giving up please don't, Every page is something to let your heart grab and hold on to. I pray this unhardens someone's heart to forgive and let something beautiful grow in the place of bitterness, hurt, pain, or whatever it is that's hindering you from flourishing. Shalawam Most High peace and blessings are upon you all.

P.S. Please make sure that we have our *heads covered* ladies, as I included a ton of bible verses, prayers, and I encourage us to study the Lord's word throughout the text. I also include activities to challenge all of us to release inner darkness and improve our own light. Elevate your thought process for changes to come.

PART I

Embody Wisdom

1

Be Encouraged

Have you ever had a day, week, or maybe even a month that you were just down? Didn't understand why? Really slothful, moody, and tired? I know I have! When you start to feel like that, *encourage yourself*.

Look in the mirror and tell yourself you're bigger than whatever it is that's pressing you. Let that negative spirit know that your *living* God is bigger. Tell yourself, "you are beautiful, Kept by someone that's Awesome, Good, Powerful, and Righteous." Ephesians 6:12 ¹²For we wrestle not against flesh and blood, but against principalities, against powers, against the rulers of the darkness of this world, against spiritual wickedness in high places. We get so caught up in the mood we get in that sometimes we forget to shake it off and keep moving.

Those negative spirits will grab us in a way that will knock us to a place where we know we don't belong. In the midst of that feeling don't forget to pray, stand still, and know that as long as we are staying in prayer that everything will be alright. It will be things that will try to bring us down, get us out of character but again remember Ephesians 6:12.

Be mindful that you have someone that wants you to win. That wants you to stay in good spirits, smiling and rejoicing because even though we fight against things we can't see we have someone that's fighting 100 times more for us. So today I'm telling you to stay encouraged no matter what, like the song says "he will make it alright but you gotta stay strong" Song: Be Encouraged by William Becton.

2

Wisdom

As we read in James 1:5 [5] If any of you lack wisdom, let him ask of God, that giveth to all men liberally, and upbraideth not; and it shall be given him.

In these times wisdom is important to have, wisdom is a part of us and our heavily Abba wants us to have it he said if we ask for it he will give it to us. Wisdom is to understand his ways and follow after them so that we may have eternal life with him. Wisdom is to get out of the ways of this world out of the darkness and walk with him in light and truth. In the bible, *the Most High* offered Solomon anything his heart desire and he ask for wisdom.

Proverbs 3:13-18 [13] Happy is the man that findeth wisdom, and the man that getteth understanding. [14] For the merchandise of it is better than the merchandise of silver, and the gain thereof than fine gold. [15] She is more precious than rubies: and all the things thou canst desire are not to be compared unto her. [16] Length of days is in her right hand; and in her left hand riches and honour. [17] Her ways are ways of pleasantness, and all her paths are peace. [18] She is a tree of life to them that lay hold upon her: and happy is every one that retaineth her.

Let us desire that amazing thing like Solomon she is such a precious gift to have.

3

Devoting Prayers

My Prayers Today are devoted to :

Friends:

Family:

Those In Need:

My Prayers Today For:

Friends:

Family:

Those In Need:

My Prayers Today For:

Friends:

Family:

Those In Need:

4

Don't Be Dismayed

Oftentimes we are dismayed. Lack of discernment brings fear that takes over us and we begin to stress. We begin to worry about things that are entirely out of our control. That's when we forget that everything is already done. For instance, a bill is due and you don't have enough money to cover it or groceries need to be put in the house, but you can't do that because of that past-due bill. Rent may be coming up, a car note, or just something major that needs to be taken care of. In this case, you can "Rob Peter to Pay Paul" as they say. Stress begins to sink in and worry begins to cover our faces. You don't want to ask anyone because you don't want anyone in your business.

Relax, take a deep breath, and let it go! Do you know the phrase let go and let God? Really let go and let God. The things we worry about are the very things that have already been taken care of, before we even have a need, the need has already been met. In these very moments, he wants us to trust him and know that we are ok because we are resting in him knowing that he is in control. Proverbs 3:5-6 [5] Trust in the Lord with all thine heart; and lean not unto thine own understanding. [6] In all thy ways acknowledge him, and he shall direct thy paths. Rest in that, how great is it to know that we don't have to understand what's going on in our lives that we are already taken care of and our needs are already met. Give yourself a sound mind, rest today, throughout the day, and tonight knowing that it is already done. Give it to him and let go understand that he did not create us to worry or fear.

Write out your thoughts and feelings below.

Try to Remember
That *the Most High* is always on time not on my time, yours, or this world's but his perfect timing again don't be dismayed.

5

Wanting Something?

Are you trying to work out the thing you want or need alone? Are you first seeking *The Most High* like the word says? Matthew 6:33 [33] But seek ye first the kingdom of God, and his righteousness; all these things shall be added unto you.

Why are you trying to do it by yourself? If we seek him first everything else will be added on to us right? Nothing that *The Most High* blesses comes back void. Whatever he says that's what it is and nothing less he is not a God that he shall lie. Pray, tell him your needs because he already knows before you even ask for it. He is just waiting for you to *SEEK HIM FIRST* so he can direct your path. If you do that then you know you have already done the 1st important thing and with his perfect provision if that door is open you know that it is a door that he opened and you will not lack anything. know that everything is on his timing. We can't pray about anything and want it to be on our time. Wait and even if it looks like nothing is happening keep your faith and move like you are already walking in your prayer. 2 Corinthians 5:7 [7] for we walk by faith, not by sight. Without that faith, it is impossible to please him. Don't worry when he has already gone ahead of you. Philippians 4:6 [6] Be careful for nothing, but in everything by prayer and supplication with thanksgiving let your requests be made known unto God.

In this space we manifest!

In this space we manifest!

Keep In Mind
Faith and fear will never share the same space.

6

Read and Reflect

Read Matthew 6

    1. What Did You Learn From It?

    2. How Can You Apply This In Your Life?

Write A Prayer:

Read Proverbs 31

    1. What Did You Learn From It?

    2. How Can You Apply This In Your Life?

Write A Prayer:

Read Isaiah 54

    1. What Did You Learn From It?

    2. How Can You Apply This In Your Life?

Write A Prayer:

Read Psalm 37

    1. What Did You Learn From It?

    2. How Can You Apply This In Your Life?

Write A Prayer:

7

Is there Room for Growth?

List 10 things you want to change
1.
2.
3.
4.
5.
6.
7.
8.
9.

10.

Always Remember
Be Mindful to accept the things you cannot change and have the power to know the difference.

List 10 things you want to change

1.

2.

3.

4.

5.

6.

7.

8.

9.

10.

8

Goal Digging

Go Ahead Dig and discover yourself! Write discoveries *below*.
What Are Your Goals?
Ask yourself what do you need to succeed?

9

What's Going on Today?

You may find a few similar featured boxes throughout the book for a *pulse check*! Make space in the space below, examine and then apply.
Ezekiel 37 1-3; [1]The hand of the Lord was upon me, and carried me out in the spirit of the Lord, and set me down in the midst of the valley which was full of bones, [2]And caused me to pass by them round about: and, behold, there were very many in the open valley; and, lo, they were very dry.[3] And he said unto me, Son of man, can these bones live? And I answered, O Lord God, thou knowest.

Today I feel?

What am I Grateful For Today?

Scriptures Or Quotes:

Prayer For Someone:

Prayer for Self:

Today I feel?

What am I Grateful For Today?

Scriptures Or Quotes:

Prayer For Someone:

Prayer for Self:

Today I feel?

What am I Grateful For Today?

Scriptures Or Quotes:

Prayer For Someone:

Prayer for Self:

Today I feel?

What am I Grateful For Today?

Scriptures Or Quotes:

Prayer For Someone:

Prayer for Self:

ENCOURAGED

10

Its Prayer Time

I take this time to pray for:

I take this time to pray for:

I take this time to pray for:

I take this time to pray for:

I take this time to pray for:

I take this time to pray for:

I take this time to pray for:

I take this time to pray for:

I take this time to pray for:

I take this time to pray for:

I take this time to pray for:

I take this time to pray for:

I take this time to pray for:

I take this time to pray for:

I take this time to pray for:

I take this time to pray for:

I take this time to pray for:

I take this time to pray for:

I take this time to pray for:

I take this time to pray for:

I take this time to pray for:

11

Strength of a Rock

My Strength?

    I Challenge Myself To?

    I Can Improve By?

    Quote Of The Day?

    My Goal For Today Is?

My Strength?

    I Challenge Myself To?

    I Can Improve By?

    Quote Of The Day?

    My Goal For Today Is?

My Strength?

I Challenge Myself To?

I Can Improve By?

Quote Of The Day?

My Goal For Today Is?

My Strength?

I Challenge Myself To?

I Can Improve By?

Quote Of The Day?

My Goal For Today Is?

My Strength?

I Challenge Myself To?

I Can Improve By?

Quote Of The Day?

My Goal For Today Is?

My Strength?

I Challenge Myself To?

I Can Improve By?

Quote Of The Day?

My Goal For Today Is?

My Strength?

I Challenge Myself To?

I Can Improve By?

Quote Of The Day?

My Goal For Today Is?

My Strength?

I Challenge Myself To?

I Can Improve By?

Quote Of The Day?

My Goal For Today Is?

My Strength?

I Challenge Myself To?

I Can Improve By?

Quote Of The Day?

My Goal For Today Is?

12

Prayer For Today

Prayer For Today.

   Repent For?

   Ask For?

   Yes, I Can do what?

Prayer For Today.

   Repent For?

   Ask For?

   Yes, I Can do what?

Prayer For Today.

   Repent For?

   Ask For?

Yes, I Can do what?

Prayer For Today.

Repent For?

Ask For?

Yes, I Can do what?

Prayer For Today.

Repent For?

Ask For?

Yes, I Can do what?

Prayer For Today.

Repent For?

Ask For?

Yes, I Can do what?

Prayer For Today.

Repent For?

Ask For?

Yes, I Can do what?

13

Self Reflection

Have you ever stopped to think maybe it's me? Maybe I'm the one that needs to get it together. Oftentimes we are so quick to blame things on others that we forget to self-examine ourselves first. Were we the problem when something occurred? Did we egg on the situation when we could have stopped it? I can't speak for anyone else but I have my moments when I'm just completely mean, and it is because I have so much on my mind and moving so fast that I get irritated about a lot of things.

Stop and self-examine yourself at all times.

What can you do to make yourself better for yourself and others, so the next time something happens and it's actually your fault? Humble yourself, if you don't know how to apologize that will help you easily begin to flow peace for you in your life. James 5:16 [16] Confess your faults one to another and pray one for another, that ye may be healed. The effectual fervent prayer of a righteous man availeth much.

When we know that we are the problem and speak to a praying man/woman about it, that person can go into prayer for you. *The Most High* said in Matthew 18:20 [20] For where two or three are gathered together in my name, there am I in the midst of them. We have time in our day to think about things. And if there is an area in your life that you need help with, acknowledge it and then move forward with that, get help so you don't hinder yourself from the blessings that have your name on it.

*Try To Remember:
Only the self-aware reflect to make it better today.

What are areas in your life where you can improve in self-examining?

14

Ten Commandments

Proverbs. 7:1-2 ¹ My son, keep my words, and lay up my commandments with thee. ² Keep my commandments, and live; and my law as the apple of thine eye. 1 John 2:4 ⁴ He that saith, I know him, and keepeth, not his commandments, is a liar, and the truth is not in him. Nothing that *the Most High* said to us comes back voided. This means he is not a man that shall lie, everything he said in his word is what it is and that's that. Which means we have to keep these at all costs.

We all say "We love him" however, a lot of people are not doing these commandments. These are very special things to do and keep, My favorite is number 4. Remember the sabbath day and keep it holy. That day is a beautiful day. Genesis 2:2-3 ² And on the seventh day God ended his work which he had made, and he rested on the seventh day from all his work which he had made. ³ And God blessed the seventh day and sanctified it: because that in it he had rested from all his work which God created and made. He's giving us permission to rest in him, renew our minds, ask for mercy, and most importantly rebuild *our spirit*. He's made it clear from the curses we are still in captivity with our oppressors and our days are stressed, in our stressful moments, we need to separate and remain holy.

All praises, glory, and honor belong to *The Most High*. Sabbath begins on 'Friday' sundown to 'Saturday' sundown learn the ends and outs give him his time, rest in him, and renew yourself.

Dig Deeper with the FASTING activity in Part 2 Let It Go.

---

*Remember:
Walk-in all these commandments daily Israel they are ours to keep.

15

Fasting

What Are You Fasting For?

> Prayer:

What Are You Fasting For?

> Prayer

What Are You Fasting For?

> Prayer

What Are You Fasting For?

> Prayer

16

Protecting Your Spirit

You ever got around someone or a group of people and felt like their energy was just off and you didn't like it. Those are the type of people that you have to keep your distance from. You don't have to dislike them but you have to know the kind of people that *the Most High* is protecting you from. We are not meant to be around everyone, people have really strong spirits that they fight every day, and being around them could very much involve you fighting their demons with them. When their spirits are aggravated with your good spirit that could shake up things that cause the enemy to step in. It is a spiritual war often people will push you to a negative space because they see a light in you and they are jealous of it.

Make sure when you are protecting your spirit that you 'Guard Your Light'. When you come across someone sit back and just watch first. Do not be so quick to jump into a conversation with them John 7:24 Judge not according to the appearance but judge righteous judgment. A lot of people probably will say that you think you are better than them because you don't want to be around them. But at the end of the day, you have to protect yourself and your spirit from people and their negative spirits.

17

Can't Stop Won't Stop

1 Thessalonians 5:17
[17] Pray without ceasing.

Let our father know I will pray until I see change...

Let our father know I will pray until I see change...

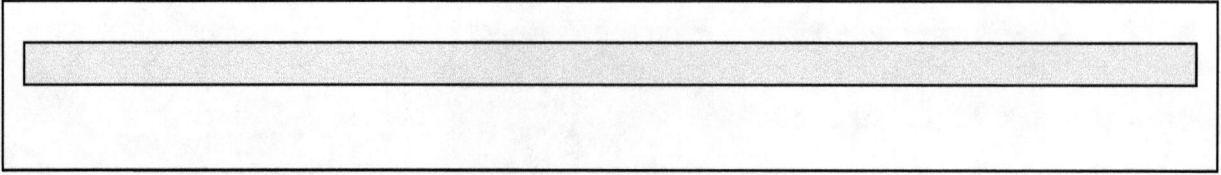

18

Gratefully Reflect

| **Today I Am Thankful For?** |
| *Example:* I am grateful for you my reader! |

| Today I Am Thankful For? |

| Today I Am Thankful For? |

| Today I Am Thankful For? |

| Today I Am Thankful For? |

| Today I Am Thankful For? |

| Today I Am Thankful For? |

| Today I Am Thankful For? |

| Today I Am Thankful For? |

19

Get Centered Prayer

Grab a pen and make it official.
What's an INTENTIONAL prayer for your soul??

20

Being Obedient

Isaiah 1:19 ¹⁹If ye be willing and obedient, ye shall eat the good of the land.

Nothing th*at The Most High* says in his word comes back void. Statues, laws, and commandments being righteous is being obedient. We are not here to just be here, we are here to make it back home to our Abba. We sometimes get caught up in the cares of this world that we forget to walk in his obedience and in reality that's all it's really about. We should be so rooted in *The Almighty* that we should want to wake up and start each day to give him his glory, praise, and to walk the way he wants us to or at least try so that we can show him that he is important to us and just like he cares for us we care for him as well.

It's just like having a child we want or would want for our child to be obedient and listen to what we say. So if we are not doing this why is it so hard for us to do so? A lot of people are scared that they will be missing out on something and the truth is nothing of this world is worth missing out on with our heavenly Abba. Let's show him daily that we love him and want to eat the good of the land, that we want all his promises, that we want to be well-pleasing unto him. Everything is for his glory even me telling yall this. ALL PRAISES TO *THE MOST HIGH!*

21

Growing Together

Let's Grow Together
What are you *planting* from the past and sowing to grow for the future?

22

Thoughts

What could I have done better today?

What could I have done better today?

What could I have done better today?

What could I have done better today?

What could I have done better today?

What could I have done better today?

What could I have done better today?

What could I have done better today?

What could I have done better today?

What could I have done better today?

What could I have done better today?

What could I have done better today?

What could I have done better today?

What could I have done better today?

What could I have done better today?

What could I have done better today?

23

Straight Way

All of us want that straight path, no twist turns, bumps, well let me just say it, no one wants the obstacles. Why not? Trials and tribulations always come to make us stronger and wiser. We never come out the same way we went in, Romans 12:12 Rejoicing in hope; patient in tribulation; continuing instant in prayer. John 16:33 These things I have spoken unto you, that in me ye might have peace. In the world ye shall have tribulation: but be of good cheer; I have overcome the world. We have to know that the only straight path should not be our mindset but *The Most High's*" tunnel vision". We have to count it as a blessing to go through things in life, not question why me? or what have I done to deserve this?

Instead, Praise him in advance, thank him for the answered prayers. Thank him for all he's getting ready to do in your life and the wisdom that you are getting ready to grab hold of. Change your view and how you are seeing your situation, realize how blessed you are, and rejoice because you know you are going to have the victory in the end. Make a joyful noise to *The Most High* and make sure you keep a sound mind.

Rather the path is to the left, right, criss-cross, crooked, or whatever he will get you where you need to be and that's where he wants you. Walk your walk and pray for the ordering of your steps and then he will guide you.

Examine what *ORDER* looks like for your life versus what it is actually?

_____

_____

What changes do you need to make versus the sacrifices are you willing to take?

_____

_____

Examine what *ORDER* looks like for your life versus what it is actually?

_____

_____

What changes do you need to make versus the sacrifices are you willing to take?

_____

_____

PART II

LET IT GO

These activities are intended for you to be real with yourself and let go and grow! Let this prayer inspire you throughout this journey.

Heavenly Father, give me the strength, Faith, and Hope to fully let go and trust that you are in full control, I give it all to you your will be done no mines. AMEN

24

Good Cry

Have you ever had one of those days or weeks when you are just aggravated? Something bad could have happened, someone could have said something out the way to you, your boss was being really mean, etc and you just held it in didn't say anything or maybe you did and it made things worse? Get somewhere alone and cry not a normal cry where tears are rolling down your face.

CRY let it all out scream, yell if you have to!

Let whatever it is that's bothering you out don't hold that sadness and anger in. It's ok to cry crying makes you feel better it cleanses you from bitterness. You are not weak if you cry. Psalm 34:17-18; [17] The righteous cry, and the Lord heareth, and delivereth them out of all their troubles [18] The Lord is nigh unto them that are of a broken heart; and saveth such as be of a contrite spirit.

When we cry especially out to him he hears us and delivers us out from whatever it is that we are going through. When we are having one of those days or weeks just know if you don't want to talk about it, cry about it to *The Most High*. He hears you, you are basically praying to our

Abba asking to make it better. You are reaching out to him for help to understand that this is not a bad thing. It says in Psalm 3:4 I cried unto the LORD with my voice, and he heard me out of his holy hill. Selah. Psalm 120:1 In my distress, I cried unto the LORD, and he heard me.

25

Write It Out

In life, it's important to have goals or you will just keep saying what you want to do and never do it. I have learned over some time to write them down. You can say what you want to do and have the thoughts of doing them but until you write them down and see them they are only thoughts.

Start with your little ones and work your way up to the big ones, getting things done that you say you want to accomplish is such a big thing even if it's small. You may be wanting to start a small business, write a book, go back to school, work on a car, or a home, whatever the case may be, write it out. Get a vision board, and set a date maybe add some pictures to help you accomplish the goal. It's ok to manifest the things you want as well, that's having faith that the things you can't see yet will happen.

When doing this you can't just sit on it *The Most High* helps those that are helping themselves. You have to meet him halfway and know as I said before tell him thy will be done, *Abba*. Thank him in advance for prosperity, abundance, grace, guidance, and new ideas. The strength to do what you are praying for and not to mistreat it when you have it.

Take a moment to write *The Most High* a **thank you** for letting you do what it is he wants you to do.

Take a moment to write *The Most High* a **thank you** for letting you do what it is he wants you to do.

*Try To Remember *
You may *never* get to do what you feel like you desire to do. According to the curses in Deuteronomy.

26

Dear self....

Write *ENCOURAGING* statements to yourself!

Example: Dear Self, *challenge* yourself to find peace in all things. You will overcome!

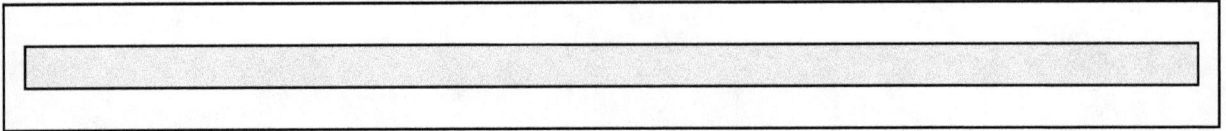

27

Write About It!

Do you have something on your mind?
Write about it below.....

28

Worrying

What does this do in your life? What does this solve? Does this make anything better or make it worse? Worrying only causes stress in your life that you do not need. John 14:27 Peace I leave with you, my peace I give unto you: not as the world giveth, give I unto you. Let not your heart be troubled, neither let it be afraid. Let go of your worrying and carry on about your day. Everything has already been written we just need to keep our eyes and heart on him because everything is already done. Worrying troubles your spirit gives you doubt and unnecessary sadness. Keep your spirits high and know that the author of your story has already done what you prayed for. Believe in him and on him so you can keep a sound mind through whatever it is that you are going through.

In life, we tend to pay attention to what the problem is not the one who will and can fix it. James 1:2-4 [2] My brethren, count it all joy when ye fall into divers temptations; [3] Knowing this, that the trying of your faith worketh patience. [4] But let patience have her perfect work, that ye may be perfect and entire, wanting nothing.
We are going to go through things, don't let the things that have come to make us better in some type of way cause us to worry. Revelation 22:13

[13] I am Alpha and Omega, the beginning and the end, the first and the last.

He has already gone ahead of us and made that thing happen. In this activity, I challenge you to point out the lack of faith.

Write down all your worries! Then identify a plan for each weakness.
Consider next that you can let go and let *The Alpha and Omega* stretch his hand.

My Strength?

   I Challenge Myself To?

   I Can Improve By?

   Quote Of The Day?

   My Goal For Today Is?

My Strength?

   I Challenge Myself To?

   I Can Improve By?

   Quote Of The Day?

   My Goal For Today Is?

29

What about your Friends?

Do you have sisters or do you have gossipy friends? There is a big difference between having those two. When your sister or " homegirl" calls are they calling to check up on you? To ask how was your day? Do you need anything? Or just to simply say hello? Or when your phone rings the first thing that you hear is girl let me tell you! Or How about such and such! No cut that out of your life ASAP a friend will not call you or come over just to gossip or dump negative things in your life. Ephesians 4:29 29 Let no corrupt communication proceed out of your mouth, but that which is good to the use of edifying, that it may minister grace unto the hearers. *The Most High* does not like gossip at all.

The more you walk with *the Most High* and grow in him, your circle will shift and so will your conversation. See when you start to elevate in your life you tend to leave some people behind and it's not a bad thing and that definitely does not make yall enemies or shouldn't have any type of bad blood with each other. It's ok to outgrow people and things when the conversation starts to make you feel like why I'm even talking to this person it's time to end that. Get you that friend that speaks life into you and the situations you are dealing with. A friend that you can pray with, study, and read with. When you speak to her or him you just know the energy is about to be great because that's what type of friend(s) you have.

I was always told "if they talk with you they will talk about you" Remember that the next time you have a conversation and ask yourself, is it positive or negative?

Dig Deeper with the RESPECTFULLY NOT TODAY activity.

Today I feel?

   What am I Grateful For Today?

   Scriptures Or Quotes.

   Prayer For Somone.

   Prayer for self.

Today I feel?

   What am I Grateful For Today?

   Scriptures Or Quotes.

   Prayer For Somone.

   Prayer for self.

30

Respectfully Not Today

In this activity, I *challenge* you to continue to examine thyself and cast out the wickedness around you.

> No drama, no gossip, no meaningless friendships, no ungodliness...
> What are you saying NO to today?

No drama, no gossip, no meaningless friendships, no ungodliness...
What are you saying NO to today?

No drama, no gossip, no meaningless friendships, no ungodliness...
what are you saying NO to today?

No drama, no gossip, no meaningless friendships, no ungodliness...
What are you saying NO to today?

No drama, no gossip, no meaningless friendships, no ungodliness...
What are you saying NO to today?

No drama, no gossip, no meaningless friendships, no ungodliness...
What are you saying NO to today?

No drama, no gossip, no meaningless friendships, no ungodliness...
What are you saying NO to today?

31

Idols

Are you on your phone a lot? Watching t.v. a lot during the day? Are you worshiping someone other than the <u>one and only</u> living God? Anything that you are giving more time than *the Most High* or praying to and it's not him you are idolizing. I mention that we should pray without ceasing 1 Thessalonians 5:17. Nothing or anyone should ever come before or over our heaven Abba or his son. John 3:16-17 [16] For God so loved the world, that he gave his only begotten Son, that whosoever believeth in him should not perish, but have everlasting life. [17] For God sent not his Son into the world to condemn the world; but that the world through him might be saved.

We have a man that sent his only son and a man that died for all of our sins. Why would we want to put anything over him? A lot of people fall short of this but asking for forgiveness and working on it would be so pleasing to him. He is very jealous and would like that alone time with you, that time over everything to show him he is worthy and more important than anything that's in your life right now. It is so important to show him how much he means to you, he gave us one heck of a sacrifice for us not to do that and to show our brother how much we love him because he had to go through it.

We are not perfect and this walk is definitely not easy, but once we know better we do better. Right? Sometimes we get caught up in life and I'm *guilty* of it, if you are doing this let's start together and STOP. On the other hand, if you are doing a great job please encourage someone to do the same.

32

Repentance

Repenting is changing, right? One thing I have learned walking this walk is that we are not perfect. We will fall short of his glory and we are going to fall Proverbs 24:16 [16] For a just man falleth seven times, and riseth up again: but the wicked shall fall into mischief.

It is so amazing to know that *The Most High* knows that we are going to fall but all he wants us to do is get back up again. Do not just fall and stay down rise back up and repent. Let me say I myself am far from perfect. I have had days when someone has made me mad and I had a few words for them, I have had days when I have been so aggravated with my job that I have been mean or rude to a co-worker

In the days that I fall short, I have to remember to pray and repent and ask for forgiveness for my words and actions. He said in his word James 1:19 [19] Wherefore, my beloved brethren, let every man be swift to hear, slow to speak, slow to wrath.

I fall short of this a lot but this is something that I know I will overcome in due time. I repent of this and ask for help with it. We all have our own flaws that we have to work on in some type of way. But as I stated above rising up, pray about it, and repent for the things you want to change and the things we have done towards ourselves, one another, and most importantly sinning against our Abba.

Matthew 3:2 [2] And saying, Repent ye: for the kingdom of heaven is at hand.

33

Forgiving Yourself

Have yall ever thought about something that you let happen to you? Something that you did to someone that they forgave you for but you still have yet to forgive yourself. Tell me, why is that? Does it make you feel some type of way when this happens? Right now, Today, STOP. Forgive yourself, and let that pain go. People speak a lot about forgiving others but what about self. Ask yourself what do you need to forgive yourself for? What are you really holding on to besides maybe guilt, anger, bitterness, or despair? The bible shows us over and over how to forgive and love our neighbor but why wouldn't he want us to forgive ourselves as well? Use the love of Christ as a mirror to love yourself as you love others.

Whatever it is that you are holding, *let it go*, it's not worth the bag it is in. It's more than likely stealing your joy along with the happiness inside of you. Stop hoarding pain inside. Stop lowering your head, ask our heavenly Abba to take it away from you. Raise your head and give yourself the strength and courage you need to forgive deep within so you can be truly at peace. Forgiveness is wrapped up in a major blessing and that is not one else's responsibility.

2 Corinthians 5:17 [17] Therefore if any man be in Christ, he is a new creature: old things are passed away; behold, all things have become new.

34

No Excuses

We all make excuses, at times for *everything*, today **no more excuses!**
What do you want to <u>stop</u> making excuses for?

PART III

SERENITY

These activities are intended to help encourage you to find *peace and acceptance.*

    SERENITY PRAYER: Philippians 4:6-7

    [6]Be careful for nothing, but in everything by prayer and supplication with thanksgiving let your requests be made known unto God. [7]And the peace of God, which passeth all understanding, shall keep your hearts and minds through Christ Jesus.

35

Healing

Understand, when you do this step, that peace will follow. Happiness will most likely overtake your spirit once healing finally occurs. Give your soul something worth holding, you owe yourself that much. The moments that hurt you in the past shouldn't still have that much control over your *right now* moments. Forgive yourself for the ones that hurt you. Ask *the Most High* to forgive you for the trespasses you did against others. Take accountability by placing responsibility back on your life, understand that you deserve to live in truth. Smile more and give people a reason to smile as well!

Pray for the restoration of the things you have lost in your life. I'm not talking about just the things you can see either. Peace of mind is security that money can't buy. It's very important to obtain and maintain. I can write these words and tell you what is what, but you have to choose to heal over everything you thought you knew. You must know that this part of you is possible.

Do you want peace?

Do you choose to be happy?

Do you desire to be loved correctly?

When you are actually healed you can give out that real love and decern it as well. Healing is also a part of inner peace, once you are able to heal or even start to heal you are starting to envision and mold your inner peace. Your spirit and mind will no longer get shaken up by negative thoughts or energy of the past because you will be able to say thank you Abba for healing me, thank you for deliverance, thank you for inner peace. If this awakening is happening now, do not fear anything other than the Most Terrible. It's never too late to choose. Please don't drag pain along with you, the days will become weeks, and before you know it, it's years down the line. You can't truly be at peace unless you go through the unrest of redemption.

Learn to heal, forgive, and be truly happy. Heal your heart and mind, believe you can only do this by prayer. By giving all woes to *The Most High* no matter the weight. Remember in Psalms 118:24 [24] This is the day which the LORD hath made; we will rejoice and be glad in it. And 1 Peter 5:7 [7] Casting all your care upon him; for he careth for you. He wants to heal us, give it to him, he's waiting for you.

Challenge yourself to heal.
Beware this is an *intimate* exercise, I encourage you the reader to endure inner peace for the better.

What areas do you need to Heal?

Who do you need to forgive?

When will you take action?

How can you start healing and forgiving?

What areas do you need to Heal?

Who do you need to forgive?

When will you take action?

How can you start healing and forgiving?

What areas do you need to Heal?

Who do you need to forgive?

When will you take action?

How can you start healing and forgiving?

What areas do you need to Heal?

Who do you need to forgive?

When will you take action?

How can you start healing and forgiving?

What areas do you need to Heal?

Who do you need to forgive?

When will you take action?

How can you start healing and forgiving?

What areas do you need to Heal?

Who do you need to forgive?

When will you take action?

How can you start healing and forgiving?

What areas do you need to Heal?

Who do you need to forgive?

When will you take action?

How can you start healing and forgiving?

36

Faith

In James 2:22 you see that his faith and his actions were working together, and his faith was made complete by what he did. His actions made his faith complete. How great is it to know if we have faith and put in our work that it is complete! Faith moves mountains. Again, we are showing him that we trust him and his process. I have been in so many situations where I couldn't do anything but have faith and keep it because we can't do anything alone and we have to know with him all things are possible.

We all have had something we wanted so bad and it was there that we put in our mind that I'm going to be alright, I'm going to keep pushing forward, I got this, I can do it! That was faith. That was your faith that moved that Mountain. *The Most High* seen you had that much faith in him to give you what you really needed in your life. Matthew 17:20 says ¹⁷ Because of your unbelief: for verily I say unto you, If ye have faith as a grain of mustard seed, ye shall say unto this mountain, Remove hence to yonder place, and it shall remove; nothing shall be impossible unto you.

Keep your faith and know that the impossible can be done in your life. Dive into the activity below by way of self-reflection and thorough evaluation of thyself.

Keep In Mind*
Faith *without* work is dead. Seeds not sowed planted can't grow.

What area of your life does your faith need to be restored?

What area of your life does your faith need to be restored?

What area of your life does your faith need to be restored?

37

Love

What is love? Is it just saying? Is it doing or is it both? To me, it's both. I don't know about anyone else but every now and then I like to hear it, oftentimes someone needs to hear it every day because they fight things mentally that they don't speak about. As the saying says "actions speak louder than words" right? Someone can say I love you and still hurt you, They can say I love you and still lie to you.

On the other hand, someone can say I love you and put every action behind that to prove that they love you. Saying it every day is an action, praying for them, showing affection hugs, kisses, a simple card, a phone call just to see how they are doing. Flowers, telling the truth, a deep conversation, and actually listening. Giving just because love is deeply caring about someone.

We all have our own definition of love, right? Now answer this, Do you love yourself? Are you caring for yourself? Are you filling yourself up with good things so you can pour that out to others? Are you taking care of your spirit and temple? Take care of yourself, love yourself, tell yourself how beautiful you are every day and how strong you are, how worthy you are, tell yourself you are enough. Remind yourself that you are the daughter of the highest and he loves you more than anything so share that love but first start with you.

38

Heartfelt Prayer

Do you have a prayer that's on your heart today one that you have been holding on to?

Well, here you go LET IT OUT...

39

Meditation

Learning this is not easy sometimes we do so much throughout the day that our mines still be going even after we try to sit still and be quiet. Learning how to get into the presence of *The Most High* and giving him that one on one time is very important. that's our time to sit and listen for anything he has to say to us or sat on our hearts.

When we stand still that allows us to do his will because we are listening for it. Psalms 19:14 says [14] Let the words of my mouth, and the meditation of my heart, be acceptable in thy sight, O LORD, my strength, and my redeemer.

Speak from your heart when you sit and commune with our heavenly *Abba* and his son. Romans 8:26 [26] Likewise the Spirit also helpeth our infirmities: for we know not what we should pray for as we ought: but the Spirit itself maketh intercession for us with groanings which cannot be uttered.

At times when we don't know what to say sitting there our spirit does. Do your part and get into his presence, pray before you do, and ask for help to quiet your mind.

I want to say if you have already been doing this keep it up this is very hard for some people to do. May the *Most High* continue to bless the pros and the beginners lol. You got this so stay with it, all he wants from us is our time and obedience he loves us so much let's return it.

40

Gratitude Prayer

Time for **Prayer!**
In this activity jot down whatever it is you are thankful for...
Go ahead and be vulnerable, be raw, as you write your testimony.

What do you feel grateful to pray about today?

Share a simple testimony?

What do you feel grateful to pray about today?

Share a simple testimony?

What do you feel grateful to pray about today?

Share a simple testimony?

41

BE Kind

Allow your tribe to express a few kind words about how they experience you.
Get your flowers while you are alive! Hear the *impact* you have on those <u>closest</u> to you.

42

Pray for Hope

Rejoicing in praise during the good and the bad, the happy and the sad. For *The Most High*, taketh all and maketh all. In this activity take serval moments to list what you are hopeful for even during times of pain.

Rejoice In Hope!

What are you hoping for?

Rejoice In Hope!

What are you hoping for?

Rejoice In Hope!

What are you hoping for?

Rejoice In Hope!

What are you hoping for?

Rejoice In Hope!

What are you hoping for?

Rejoice In Hope!

What are you hoping for?

Rejoice In Hope!

What are you hoping for?

43

Flow

I want to say to keep moving forward! Please don't let the cares of this world stop you from seeing the love that is in front of you.

Find some time in your busy schedule. May just be an hour or so for you to give yourself a mental break. By relaxing or just doing something you really love to do. It's okay to give yourself that time to be alone. Conduct your spirit for the will of *The Most High* no matter the chaos around you. Always take a moment to let the energy flow.

I hope you enjoyed this journal and can reflect back on some of these entries and smile. Smile because of how much you *embody wisdom* and learned to *let it out* and managed to find *serenity*. Perhaps just look back on a prayer that you realized was received. Maybe just reflect on how you increased your faith in The *Most High* by study and doing the necessary hard work to heal.

I love you all and remember to keep pushing and never give up on yourself and living in the truth.

Resources

Holy Bible King James Version with Apocrypha -1611

https://unsplash.com/

www.ingramcontent.com/pod-product-compliance
Lightning Source LLC
Chambersburg PA
CBHW062022090426
42811CB00005B/927